Every Ending is a New Beginning

(The Journey from Breaking Up to Moving On)

By Kevin Darné

About the Author

Kevin Darné is the author of <u>My Cat Won't Bark! (A Relationship Epiphany).</u> *My Cat Won't Bark!* is about learning how to approach relationships with complete awareness, having realistic expectations, and using self-empowerment techniques. It is laced with several humorous anecdotes and has received noteworthy positive editorial reviews from the likes of Publishers Weekly, Reader's Favorite, and Midwest Book Review.

Kevin is also the author of <u>Online Dating Avoid the Catfish!: How to Date Online Successfully.</u> *Avoid the Catfish!* is for anyone who wants to take control of their online dating endeavors.

"It's not that online dating sucks, too many people suck at online dating!"

Avoid the Catfish! is a must read for anyone considering using an online dating site or app!

In March of 2020, Kevin published <u>Pump Your Brakes! How To Stop Having Bad First Dates.</u> This book is designed to help readers keep things in perspective when it comes to first dates. Dating is supposed to be a *fun* sociable activity. This is especially true of a *first* date. The book is packed with dos and don'ts, along with how to deal with *ghosting* and finding your *ideal mate.*

Kevin's dating insight has been featured on WGN-TV Morning News Chicago, The Chicago Tribune, NBCNews.com, Cosmopolitan.com, Askmen.com, ReadersDigest.com, Bravotv.com, Match.com, Zoosk.com, Tinder, PsychologyToday.com, Men'sHealth.com, Bustle.com, Babble.com, Romper.com, AARP.org, Redbookmag.com, along with many other digital publications and radio appearances. For more information visit Lovealert911.com

Reviving Hearts with Awareness & Self-Empowerment!

"Never love anyone who treats you like you're ordinary."
– Oscar Wilde

Contents

Introduction

Before we dive into *Every Ending is a New Beginning*, I believe it's important to tell you what this book is *not* about. It's not about *playing the blame game* with exes, finding ways to get even with them, or creating a strategy to get back with your ex.

It's about accepting the fact that the relationship is *over* and *moving on* with your life. This is just the end of *one chapter* in your book of life. Your future lies ahead of you and not behind you!

Therefore, if there is any part of you which secretly hopes for a magical reconciliation and a *happily ever after ending* with your ex; this book is definitely *not* for you!

Over the years, I have often been asked why is it so difficult for people to move on after a breakup. In order to *move on,* we have to *let go.* Oftentimes people don't actually *want* to let go. Simply put, you can't get to second base if you insist upon keeping one foot on first base.

Throughout this book, we're going to examine breakups from different points of view. Quite often, when there is a discussion regarding breakups, many of us assume the role of the person who was *dumped* rather than imagining ourselves in the position of the person delivering the news. It's much easier to empathize with the person who is shocked or caught off guard.

Nevertheless, there is often some hand wringing and tension for the person ending a relationship. Almost anyone who has had a good amount of dating experience has been put in the position of having to inform a partner the relationship is no longer meeting their needs or there are issues and differences which for the foreseeable future are too difficult to accept or compromise on. Subsequently, I have chosen to also include a chapter consisting of a *breakup method.*

Ultimately, it does not matter who, why, where, when or how a relationship concludes. The end result is still the same. You are once again single, free, and available to find Mr. or Ms. Right.

Every ending is a new beginning!

When it Comes to **Love and Relationships,** Most of Us *Fail Our Way* to Success.

Practice Relationships

The vast majority of us will experience multiple breakups and possibly divorce in our lifetime. Rarely is someone's "first love" their *last* love. We're simply too immature or naïve to understand this truth, especially during our youth. Many of us during that period also lack the ability to mentally project ourselves into the future. *Right now,* is all that matters to us which creates immense urgency and pressure. It also makes it difficult to put things into perspective.

When I was in Jr. high, there was a thirteen-year-old girl who attempted suicide because her fourteen-year-old boyfriend broke up with her in order to date the new girl in school. No thirteen-year-old girl should think her life isn't worth living and no fourteen-year-old boy should be responsible for the wellbeing of another person.

I have often wondered over the years how this woman may have reflected on that incident as she got older, graduated from high school, went to college, got married and possibly had her own daughter reach the age of thirteen and seeing her child have a crush on a boy at school.

With age and life experience comes wisdom. Parents around the world oftentimes attempt to get their teenagers to focus on school and avoid getting too wrapped up in dating and relationships. Based upon their own life experience, they're fully aware the teenage years are among the most vulnerable periods in our lives because we tend to give all of ourselves and have unrealistic expectations. We ignored our parents' warnings and their efforts to protect us from heartache. Oftentimes, it's not until we have teenagers of our own that we come to appreciate the wisdom our parents were trying to impart. They knew our teenage relationships were destined to fail.

The following are examples of actual unedited postings in a dating forum.

"So, my ex (F/20) broke up with me (M/20) around 3 months ago after dating for about 4 years and it's really starting to chew at me. We started dating in high school and she was my first girlfriend, well to be more exact *my first everything*, whereas I wasn't close to being her first anything. We met through a mutual friend of ours and hit it off straight away through our mutual love of art and anime. I was told before though that she was not loyal, (nice way of saying it) and that I shouldn't get too attached, but me being me, I prefer to experience things for myself. We started dating about 2 months after getting to know each other and in all honesty the main reason was because I was thinking with my *second head,* she's charming, beautiful has a sense of humor can hold a conversation, smart and creative, all the right things a person wants right? But in our first month she cheated twice if not three times.

"Since it was my first time I didn't really pick up on the red flags, or I did, but brushed them aside because I thought maybe a little more love would fix things, and it did! She slowly stopped and eventually became my other half. We spent more or less all of our time together getting to know each other.

"Over the three years we dated on and off, spoke, ignored each other became friends, dated then repeated the cycle but we never really strayed far from each other, but that changed this year it seems like this time she really wanted to end stuff between us and I'm still trying to figure out why. One moment we're discussing potential marriage and even maybe adoption (we decided that since she doesn't want to risk another miscarriage, but I still want kids) and all that.

Currently I'm okay with her decision to not have contact, and I will continue to respect that decision, but there are times where I'm up late just thinking of her and the heart starts to ache and stuff like that, or I'm listening to music and my vision blurs with tears from thoughts of her. Any advice on how to not completely crumble because of this? How do you move on or forget the first person you really love?" – S. Sabo"

I wrote the following response to his request for advice.

In all honesty, almost no one meets their *soulmate* at age 16 in these modern times. Odds were against you two ever spending the next 60-70 years living a "happily ever after life."

When it comes to love and relationships, most of us *fail our way* to success. Rarely does anyone hit a homerun their 1st, 2nd, 3rd, or 4th time up at bat. If this were not the case, we would all be married to our high school sweethearts!

Our teenage years and early twenties are generally a time of exploring and learning. All of those relationships are essentially "practice relationships." With each failure, betrayal, and heartache, we are presented with an opportunity to either craft or refine our mate selection/ screening process and *must haves list* for choosing our future mates in our adult relationships.

The reason why you didn't break up with your girlfriend after she cheated on you three times was because you were "all in" and this was your *first* relationship. You were immature and had unrealistic expectations for the relationship to begin with. However, you are likely going to come to a point where having someone cheat on you in future relationships *will be* a "deal breaker."

You won't be as gullible or naïve as you were during your first relationship. Anyone with an ounce of self-esteem has boundaries and "deal breakers." Each of us establishes our own.

The reason why it's so hard for a lot of people to move on after a breakup is because they really don't want to! What they are really hoping for is a *magical reconciliation* with their ex.

In order to *move on,* you have to want to *let go.* The first step is to accept the relationship is really over. The next step is enacting the "no contact rule." It's simply unrealistic to expect to go from being "red hot lovers" to "instant platonic friends" resembling siblings. Your ex is the last person who can help you get over her!

You should put away all mementos from the relationship. Block phone numbers and email addresses, unfriend her on social media, and avoid going to places you know your ex frequents.

Grieve among your close friends and family, refocus your attention on education or career objectives, work-out, become more active with hobbies and other interests. At some point, you'll meet other girls you're attracted to and engage in casual dating. You'll eventually find someone you want to be exclusive with. That's how it usually works. No one ever *forgets* their *first love.*

However, your future lies ahead of you and not behind you. Bear in mind that in order for your *ex* to have been "the one" *she* would have had to see *you* as being "the one." At the very least, a "soulmate" is someone who actually wants to be with you!

"A bend in the road is not the end of the road unless you fail to make the turn." - Helen Keller

"Never love anyone who treats you like you're ordinary." - Oscar Wilde

You may want to read: <u>My Cat Won't Bark! (A Relationship Epiphany)</u>, <u>Online Dating Avoid the Catfish! How to Date Online Successfully</u>, and <u>Pump Your Brakes! How to Stop Having Bad First Dates</u>. All three books are a quick read and offer lots of sound dating and relationship advice. The world may not owe you anything but *you* owe yourself the world!

Best wishes!

The following request for advice comes from an eighteen-year-old woman dating an eighteen-year-old man while attending different universities. It is a common dilemma for young lovers.

My boyfriend [18M] and I [18F] are going to different colleges halfway across the world:

"We have been dating for about 10 months, and although I'm young and I suppose I don't really know what love is, this is what I think it is. We are going to different schools; I'm staying on the west coast and he's going to the east coast. He said before that he didn't want to do long distance and I agreed, but it made me think that if he isn't willing to fight for it, does he really care as much as he says he does? I'm not so sure I could do long distance either as I think we would both be unhappy being unable to see each other but this thought keeps nagging at the back of my head that our relationship must not be worth as much as I think it is if either of us aren't willing to fight to make it work.

"I am trying to just cherish our last month together but I guess I am becoming kind of bitter. He has the option to stay in our city instead of moving away for school because it's all online and it would make sense in terms of safety and coronavirus but he is choosing to go anyways. I, on the other hand, have chosen to stay in our city because the state my college is in is doing very poorly in terms of coronavirus, dorms are mad expensive, and everything's online anyway. I could never be so selfish as to ask him to stay simply for me but some part of me feels kind of bitter or hurt that he is choosing to leave. It also hurts because my friend who is also in a relationship was facing the same problem with her boyfriend going to a different school far away but they ended up both deciding to stay at home and I guess I am jealous of that. Any advice?" – V. H.

My response is as follows:

Every fall, millions of high school sweet-hearts go away to different universities vowing to maintain a long-distance relationship for the next 4-6 years while pursuing their degrees. They are too naïve and immature to realize how unrealistic they are being. What normally happens after one or two semesters one or both of them eventually make new friends on campus, attend various events, including dances and parties, possibly pledge a fraternity or sorority and eventually find themselves liking someone who is on campus. Oftentimes, what happens is there is a *breakup call* made or someone gets busted for cheating.

Their real crime, however, was their immature act of making an unrealistic promise in the first place. Long-distance relationships were meant to be temporary. The goal is to be with the person you love. Whenever there is no realistic light at the end of the tunnel whereby someone will be relocating to be with the other, couples usually drift apart.

It is the counting down of the months, weeks, and days until one is finally done with the inconvenience of being in a long-distance relationship that keeps it strong!

You stated you both agreed you didn't want to be in a long-distance relationship. Give yourselves credit for being very practical and mature for your age.

Make the most of your last month together and if it's meant to be, somewhere down the line, you might end up back in the same town and get back together. There's a whole new world waiting for you. Teenage love is just one chapter in your book of life.

"Worrying doesn't empty tomorrow of its sorrow, it empties today of its strength."
- Corrie Ten Boom

Neither good times nor bad times last forever.

Understanding that *right now* isn't forever is a difficult concept to embrace when you're in the middle of going through a breakup and trying to heal. However, we must find a way to acknowledge that we are not the first nor the last to have to deal with heartache. Whether we want to hear it or not, it's important to know others have survived and gone on to thrive after being dumped or having to end a relationship. The following is a post from one such person.

It's been one year, life is good

"Today marks one full year of no contact with the girl that left me for another guy after a 5-year relationship (I am 24M). It destroyed me. Getting over it was one of the hardest things I ever had to do but I did it. I was over it at about the 4-month mark and now I don't even think about it.

"I have finally had the opportunity to test the waters and indeed there are many fish in the sea! Anybody who is recovering from a tough breakup, you *will* get past it and find that more than one person finds you desirable. When someone leaves you for someone else, it's easy to think "well if she didn't want me, nobody will" and I've had quite a few dates since the break up and it feels great. Not all are winners but some are and lead into either a soon-to-be relationship or a friendship if the chemistry is off.

     Practice Relationships

"Now I also know you might think of me keeping the breakup date in my mind weird but I thought of it as the day the old me died and I was reborn. I made this post for anybody who feels undesirable, going through a breakup or dating in general. By no means am a "ladies' man", I do have spurts of loneliness as well. But being single for the first time in 5 years really forced me to learn how to love and live with myself instead of depending on someone else to help me be happy. Over these past 12 months I have gotten into the best physical shape of my life, I completely stopped taking any anxiety medication and have picked up a ton of new hobbies I had put on the back burner due to having less time because of being in a relationship.

"To everybody reading this, you got this. You just have to keep putting one foot in front of the other. It doesn't have to be giant steps but they have to be moving forward.

If I can do it, anybody can." – **G. T.**

As you can see from doing the math, G.T. met his ex when he was 18 years old and they broke up when he was 23. It has now been a year since the split and he is 24 today.

The more dating and relationship experience we have, the better we are able to put breakups in the right perspective. Finding our ideal mate is an *exploratory process* which is bound to contain mistakes in our mate selection process along the way. Life really does go on.

"Parents were the only ones obligated to love you; from the rest of the world, you had to earn it." - Ann Brashares

The Unconditional Love Myth

Throughout history, we have romanticized the idea of commitment to mean no matter what happens our relationship will remain intact. No one on their wedding day imagines getting divorced. Nevertheless, the words, "Until death do us part," come with a few caveats.

Everyone, at some point, wants to be in a secure relationship. The kind of relationship where one emphatically feels at last their heart has found a home. For some people, it's believing things will never change. Stability and predictability provide feelings of comfort and security.

Home

Robert Frost once stated, "Home is the place where, when you have to go there, they have to take you in." Home is also the place where you let your hair down, kick off your shoes, relax, and be your "authentic self." We say what we want and do what we want without concerning ourselves with being "politically correct." Home is the place where you're free to be *you*. Billy Sunday said, "Home is the place we love best and grumble the most."

Romanticism

For many people, being at home in a relationship or marriage means *unconditional love*. No matter what one says or does they feel assured their mate will never abandon them. There will be laughter and tears throughout the years but at the end of day when it's all said and done, they will find themselves in each other's arms. Breaking up or getting divorced are simply not options.

Contradiction

The problem with holding onto these definitions of home and the romanticism of unconditional love is each of us has an ego and certain *must haves* or requirements. We want our mates to be considerate of our feelings. We want to be respected, appreciated, and adored by our significant others. A person who says whatever comes to their mind without using an "edit button" or taking into account their mate's feelings is not likely to be in that relationship for very long especially if their partner has any self-esteem. Many of us also do not want a doormat for a mate. We expect and respect people that have boundaries and deal breakers. Therein lies the unconditional love contradiction. Having boundaries and deal breakers means there *are* conditions.

Deal Breakers

The most common examples of "unconditional love" are often attributed to God's love for mankind and a parent's love for their child, especially a mother's love.

Everyone else has "deals breakers," whether it's verbal/physical abuse, cheating, financial irresponsibility, compulsive lying, hidden addictions such as gambling, drinking, drugs, and pornography. Deal breakers are boundaries or a "line in the sand" which serves to measure how much value we place on ourselves, the relationship, and those we are involved with. To knowingly commit an act which your mate considers to be one of their "deal breakers" says a lot about how much you care about them. Most people *in love* do not intentionally hurt their mate.

Loving in Reverse

Quite a few people practice loving in reverse. In other words, they subscribe to the notion of bending over backwards to please someone *new* whom they are attracted to in order to win them over. They remove the word *no* from their vocabulary. They agree to every suggestion this person makes. Odds are both people are behaving the same way which leads them to believe they have found their "soul-mate." After there is an emotional investment and time goes by, there is an expectation that giving one's best is *no longer a requirement* to maintain the relationship. We make ourselves "at home" and *relax*. In fact, the longer the relationship lasts the less concerned we become with our appearance or pleasing them. If for some reason the relationship ends, we go back to being on our "best behavior" in order to *attract* a new person. One would think we'd be much kinder to someone who has been with us through the ups and downs over the years than someone we are trying to get to know. We treat *the new* better than *the tried and true*.

Unconditional Love

Aside from God's love of mankind and a mother's love for her child, the only real unconditional love left is the love we have for ourselves. No one else is going to stay with you forever if you don't make them feel special, loved, and appreciated. Long-term relationships come with a price. Both people have to put in the effort to nurture the relationship. You have to respect and value one another. However, most importantly, you have to understand no one is *stuck* with anyone. Everyone has "deal breakers." Unless one lacks self-esteem, unconditional love is a myth!

"While we are free to choose our actions, **we are not free to choose the consequences** of our **actions.**" – Stephen R. Covey

Three Reasons Why Couples Break Up

A lot of speculation has been made over the years to determine why relationships and marriages fail. No matter how long the list of reasons is, most fall under the heading of three categories.

They Chose the Wrong Mate (They're too incompatible)

Each of us chooses our own friends, lovers, and spouse. Oftentimes people decide to enter into an exclusive relationship or marriage without fully knowing if they share the same values, want the same things for a relationship, naturally agree on how to obtain those things, and last but not least, have a mutual depth of love and desire for each other.

As stated previously, during the *infatuation phase* of a new relationship both people tend to bend over backwards to impress each other. The word *no is* seldom if ever heard. Neither person wants to say or do anything which might *blow it* with the new object of their affection. Conversations and laughter flow easily. Token gifts and cards are given "just because" and sex is spontaneous and passionate. Everything one person wants to do the other is game for. It's only natural for an inexperienced dater to believe they have found their "soulmate."

However, it's not until an emotional investment has been made or people feel secure enough not to fear their mate will automatically walk away from a relationship that they start to relax and reveal their "authentic selves." The word *no* isn't so foreign to the ear anymore.

Major disagreements and misunderstandings reveal each other's expectations, boundaries, and "deal breakers" within the relationship. You might even discover your mate never liked certain things you believed you had in common. You may even feel like a victim of bait and switch.

It's almost a cliché to hear someone say: "He or she is not the same person I fell in love with!" Naturally, every relationship will have its share of disagreements and misunderstandings, but when it becomes apparent someone has to *change their core being* in order to make a relationship "work," there is a good chance they have chosen the *wrong* person for a partner.

There is no amount of *communication* or *work* which can overcome being with someone who simply does *not* want what *you* want. Compatibility trumps compromise. Like attracts like and opposites attract divorce attorneys! Life is too short to be trying to change water into wine. The goal is to find someone who *already is* what you want.

Several years ago, I shared the aforementioned philosophy with a class and a young-lady stated, "I want to be with someone who will *challenge me* and *make me grow.*"

Apparently, peace and serenity in a relationship isn't for everyone. Some people would be bored with it. However, something tells me as they get older, they may come to appreciate natural compatibility. Personally speaking, when I return to the castle after a full day of slaying dragons, I just want to take off the amour, put down the sword and shield. The last thing I want is *another challenge.* I have all the challenges I want on the other side of my front door!

Some people measure their partner's love by how much they are willing to sacrifice, be inconvenienced, or engage in an activity he or she does not enjoy in order to please them. Anyone who derives joy at watching their mate be unhappy causes me to question *their* love.

At some point, a person gets tired of always being wrong, fighting, jumping through hoops, and trying to be someone *they are not* in order to keep their mate happy or expecting them to change. If you can't be yourself, you're never going to be happy. Couples who enjoy each other's company and agree on most things are usually happier than those who don't. *Who knew?!*

A Deal Breaker was Committed

Anyone with an ounce of self-esteem has boundaries and "deal breakers." Deal breakers are in the eye of the beholder and they vary from person to person. There is no such thing as a universal deal breaker. Whatever you or I could come up with, there are likely people who are living under those conditions who have no plans of ever walking away from their relationship or marriage. Nevertheless, most people draw a line in the sand whereby they will not tolerate certain behavior.

The most common deal breakers are cheating/infidelity, verbal/physical abuse, engaging in criminal behavior, drug/alcohol/gambling/porn addition, emotional/physical neglect, financial irresponsibility which causes hardship on the household, and being taken for granted.

Deal breakers may be spontaneous and unforeseen situations that arise without warning. One never truly knows how they are going to react until they are placed in situations. There is a big difference between discussing a *hypothetical scenario* and encountering it in *real life*. A lot of people for example proclaim cheating to be an "automatic deal breaker" and yet many of them choose to go to therapy in an attempt to save their marriages and keep their household intact.

In some instances, people offer forgiveness to their mate but later realize they simply can't get past the offense. No matter how transparent their partner is, along with all the effort they make to change or walk the straight and narrow path, the person who was hurt keeps reliving the incident. Eventually, they conclude that they need to move on in order to have a chance at finding happiness.

They Fell Out of Love or Stopped Wanting the Same Things

In any relationship, over time, we are either *growing together* or *growing apart*. Communication is the GPS for relationships. It lets us know which direction we are heading in. Falling out of love can be a slow gradual hardly noticeable occurrence. Maybe the couple had children and made them their top priority. They put romance and passion on the "back burner." Another possibility is one or both people put the bulk of their energy into establishing a career. Their marriage or relationship feels more like they are siblings or platonic companions than lovers. While one person is completely content with the way things are, the other wants them to make more effort to put the *magic* back into the relationship. However, after observing their partner's lack of enthusiasm or enduring a series of rejections they eventually give up trying. Relationships are like gardens; if you nurture them, they thrive and if you neglect them, they die.

In some instances, a person may come to examine their life and decide they want to make some major changes which their partner never signed up for. Whether it's a mid-life crisis or *mid-life awakening,* most people reach an age where they realize they have more years behind them than in front of them. Suddenly they are recalling dreams they may had given up on or find themselves creating "bucket lists" in an attempt to give their later years some zest and adventure.

Imagine coming home from work to find your spouse suggesting you both quit your jobs, sell the house, and cash out your 401ks to buy a RV and travel back and forth across the country. Depending on how badly one person wants to do something, it can lead to a breakup or divorce. Ultimately, when it's all said and done, life is a *personal* journey. While it may take two people to make a relationship work, it only takes one person to want out in order for it to fail.

Why Communication and Therapy Often Fail

Although many people are quick to state that communication is the key to solving issues in relationships, the reality is, a lot of folks have bought into the "soulmate myth." According to the "soulmate myth," *your soulmate will instinctively know what to do or say to please you.* It's very common to hear someone say to their partner: "I shouldn't have to *ask* or *tell* you…etc." Never mind the fact that asking will likely to increase their odds of getting it. Most people want their mate to show consideration by coming up with the idea *on their own*. Getting what they want after asking for it is not considered romantic. It may also leave a bitter taste of resentment.

When it comes to couples' therapy, many couples do not go until after one of them has clearly *checked out* of the relationship. The sessions end up being just a box to check off on the list before heading to divorce court. They can now tell their family and friends they *tried therapy*.

Beware of Trial Separations

Sometimes couples consider taking a "break" or having a trial separation. Rarely is this a mutual decision. Oftentimes, it's simply a ploy by the person who is leaning towards ending the relationship but doesn't want their partner to completely freak out, or they want to test the waters being single again before they announce they want out of the relationship or marriage.

Living in Limbo

When you have a partner tell you they need space or want time away, what they're saying is they want to determine if they would be happier if you were not around. Nevertheless, in some situations, they still want you to behave as if you're a couple. It's a breakup with rules.

 Three Reasons Why Couples Break Up

In other instances, someone may have a person in mind they want to date or pursue. From their point of view if they have sex with someone else it's not cheating because they were on a break. It is not unheard of for "break babies" to be conceived while couples are apart.

I have known more than one married couple who have been separated for over twenty years and neither person ever bothered to file for divorce until one of them decided they wanted to get married to someone else. Trial separations without a deadline are messy.

Logically, it makes no sense to keep a bag packed by the front door in the event a major issue arises in your relationship or marriage. The more *practice breakups* a couple has, the easier it becomes to have the final breakup. Not many couples can resolve issues in their relationship or marriage while being apart. A <u>research study</u>, conducted at Ohio State University reports 79% of couples who separate eventually divorce. A trial separation without therapy is very likely to fail.

Your future lies **ahead** of you **not** behind **you.**

How to Move On

A very common topic in dating forums is that of seeking advice for how to move on after a breakup. Many people will come right out and ask: Why is it so hard to move on?

The truth of the matter is, most people who ask that question really don't *want to* move on. What they would really like to happen is to find a way to get back with their ex or have him or her come crawling back to them and beg for forgiveness. Sometimes people get hung up on how the breakup went down and they can't get past what was or was not said.

In the era we live in, it is becoming more common for people to text breakup announcements or elect to simply *ghost* someone they were dating without ever providing a reason.

While some people love to engage in debates over the right or wrong way for ending a relationship, the simple truth is that all breakups are done at the comfort level of the person who wants out of the relationship. Just as being let go by an employer, you don't have any say in how, where, or when. The only thing you can control is how you react to being fired or dumped.

Anger is the Mask that Hurt Wears

No one likes to be dismissed especially without seeing any warning signs. Ordinarily level headed normal people have been known to explode in anger, threaten to blackmail, or become violent upon learning the person they've devoted time and emotion to suddenly wants out. Taking such actions as constantly calling, texting, or dropping by to demand a better explanation or to seek closure, can lead to being arrested and charged with harassment or stalking.

Our ego sometimes has a difficult time accepting the fact we have been dumped especially when it appears to come without any warning. In other instances, we are the ones ending the relationship which has its own challenges to contend with which will be discussed in a later chapter. The following steps are to help you move on. Some of it repeats previous passages.

Accept It is Over

As long as one holds out hope of getting back with their ex, they will never truly move on. In fact, many of us tend to think the most romantic love stories involve couples who broke up and get back together. In several movies, boy meets girl, boy screws up, boy begs girl to take him back, girl eventually takes him back and they live happily ever after.

We come to expect the person who dumped us or caused us to end the relationship to regret their actions and realize how lucky they were to have us. Nothing makes a girl feel more special than having a guy beg her to take him back. In her eyes, there is no mountain too high, no valley too low, or river too wide for him to conquer in order to get back into her good graces.

There are also countless hit songs that involve men asking for forgiveness and second chances. It's not unusual for a girl with a broken heart to hear a friend say, "Girl, trust me, he'll be back."

Investing time waiting by the phone to get a call, text, or email from an ex keeps you from moving on. It also doesn't help if you have a history of breaking up and getting back together. Couples who have been on and off again may view their breakups as being temporary.

When the call never comes or one learns their ex is dating someone else it finally hits them that this time it might truly be over. Allowing your ex to determine your future is disempowering. There are also those who take matters into their own hands by trying to get their ex back.

A Google search of: "How to get your ex back?" will reveal a whole list of articles, books, videos, workshops, and even "magic spells" designed to help one get back with their ex. Having a desire to be with someone who does *not* want to be with you can be an exercise of self-torture.

Loneliness and having bad dating experiences after a breakup can cause one to romanticize the past. It's easy to slip on a pair of rose-tinted glasses and engage in a selective trip down memory lane whereby you only recall the "good times" you shared with your ex. Nostalgia is the equivalent of a fog in the brain. It keeps one from thinking clearly.

Holidays and birthdays coupled with seeing couples in happy relationships can tempt one to pick up the phone and unintentionally start down the path of becoming a "booty call" or creating a "friends with benefits" scenario that gives them false hope for a possible reconciliation. Once they realize it was only sex to their ex, it almost feels as if they were dumped again.

In order for your ex to have been "the one," *he* or *she* would have had to see *you* as being "the one." At the very least, a "soulmate" is someone who actually wants to be with you!

Put Away Mementos

It's impossible to truly move on if you are surrounded by photos of your ex and other things which remind you of times you shared together. It's not necessary to throw these things away but in order to have a real chance at moving on and finding a new love, you have to make room.

Grieve Among Friends and Family

Your inner circle of close friends and family help to provide you with emotional security. Shutting out the world rather than talking with those who know you best can lead to depression. Everyone has experience with having a failed relationship or rejection. It gets better with time. In the event you do not have close friends and family, consider counseling as a way to release pain.

Enact the No Contact Rule

It is a common fallacy to believe by staying connected to an ex proves you're *mature* or the *bigger person*. You have nothing to prove to your ex!

It's unrealistic to expect to go from being "red hot lovers" to "instant platonic friends" resembling siblings. Blocking phone numbers, email addresses, and unfriending on social media is recommended. Your ex is the last person who can help you get over them and vice versa.

The opposite of love is not hate, its *indifference.* When seeing or hearing from your ex no longer stirs up any emotion in you, that is when you'll know you are truly over him or her.

The best friendships between exes usually occur after a *large gap in time* whereby both people have found love and happiness with new mates. One day they bump into each other and exchange email addresses and decide to touch base from time to time.

Some exes really do not want you to get over them. They behave like zombies. Every time you start to feel like you're in a good place, they pop up out of nowhere to see if you're still holding a warm spot in your heart for them. It feeds their ego to know they *could* get you back.

Closure is Overrated

There is nothing your ex could do or say that would make you feel better about having your heart broken in two. Some people believe getting feedback from their ex will help them in their future relationships. However, there are two things they fail to consider.

The first is that it makes no sense for you to change for your ex. Secondly, the very thing that drove them away could be the same reason why the next person you date falls madly in love with you! Ultimately, the goal is to find someone who will love and appreciate you for who *you* are.

Refocus on Yourself

Breakups and divorces can be cathartic if one sets aside time to do some introspective thinking and reexamine their life overall. You may have been neglecting hobbies, dreams, friendships, career goals, and other aspects of your life while you were in your last relationship. It is not uncommon for some people to start working out, traveling, and rediscovering themselves.

Get Out There!

It is extremely difficult to attempt to *forget someone* without *replacing them* in some way. Simply put, a new thought replaces an old thought. Dating, companionship, sex, and having experiences with someone *new* is the last hurdle to clear in order to get over an ex.

Fortunately, we live in an era where there are more tools for meeting *new people* than ever before. It is far easier today to be *proactive* rather than having to rely on chance meetings when it comes to finding new people to socialize with or date. Don't be a passenger in your own life. Take the wheel!

There are online dating sites and apps, social media sites, and Meetup.com which has numerous types of hobby groups made up of people with shared interests. Singlescruise.com offers Caribbean cruises specifically designed for singles to meet, mingle, and have fun. Once Covid-19 issues are addressed, you'll have lots of options for meeting new people.

Sometimes, just traveling alone or with a single friend gets the juices flowing. People on vacation always seem to be a bit bolder than at home. Nightclubs, hotel lounges with live entertainment, and bars, are places where many single people still go to meet others and let their hair down.

Metropolitan and suburban areas offer outdoor festivals, parks, beaches, happy hours in local restaurant bars after work, along with gatherings and parties your co-worker and friends' host.

Another often overlooked place to meet quality people is volunteering to work for or attend high profile charitable events. In order to meet the type of people you want to be with *you have to run in their same circles*. Knowing what *you want* should dictate *where* you shop.

Simply make up your mind to go out, flirt, and have a great time. People who are positive and happy with their life tend to attract others. Those who come across as standoffish usually repel people. The world may not owe you anything but *you* owe yourself the world!

Reality Check

That man or woman you now feel like you can't live without, just know this; there are billions of women and men who are doing exactly that every single day. In fact, *you* use to be one of us! Remember you had a *life* before you met your ex! This is just one chapter in your book of life.

"Some people come into our life as blessings. Some come in your life as lessons."

– Mother Teresa

"**Being with** no
one **is better**
than **being with
the** wrong one."
- Anonymous

The Breakup Method

For a variety of reasons, sometimes we are the ones who have to initiate a breakup discussion. Whenever we determine our needs are not being met in a relationship and realize our partner is incapable of being the kind of person we want or need, oftentimes, the best option is to move on.

Attempting to change someone usually leads to frustration on our part and resentment on the part of our mate. There are very few people walking around with one hand raised in the air screaming: "I'm looking for someone to change me!"

Most people want to be loved and appreciated for who *they* are. There is no amount of *communication* or *work* which can overcome being with someone who does *not* want what you want. You basically have two options and they are to continue to stay where you are suffering or turn the page and start a new chapter. Some people believe divorce or breaking up is the easy way out. However, anyone who has actually gone through a divorce can tell you, getting married is a lot easier than going through a divorce!

Couples who were never married but were in long-term relationships or possibly cohabitated also experience the combination of a sense of loss and fear of uncertainty which comes with starting over. It takes more courage to face an unknown future than it does to stay put in a known present.

Whether it's a decision to get a divorce or a breakup initiating the conversation can be stressful. It is generally presumed that being dumped is *hard* and breaking up with someone is *easy*. Anyone who has ever initiated a breakup, divorce, or fired someone, is keenly aware of the stress that builds up during the days and nights leading up to the conversation. Countless times, one goes over possible scenarios in their mind to prepare them self for potential reactions. The following are some recommended steps designed to help you get through the breakup process.

Think

The first thing you need to do is some serious introspective thinking as well as reflecting on the relationship in order to determine if you *genuinely* are ready to call it quits for good. Breaking up should be thought of as being just as serious as taking wedding vows. You don't want to create a yo-yo relationship whereby you breakup one day and call to makeup the next day. One of the best methods for making a tough decision was said to have been originated by Ben Franklin.

Take a sheet of paper and draw a line down the center. On the left side of the paper, use the heading (pros) and on the right side of the paper, use the heading (cons). Begin to list the pros and cons for staying in the relationship. On another sheet of paper, you might do the same thing for traits you desire in a mate versus traits your significant other possesses. The goal is to get everything in black and white. This will also help crystalize the reasons why you want to end the relationship. Being honest with yourself helps you to stick with a decision.

Plan

After you have thought things through and have decided that it would be best for you to break up, the next step is to plan your exit. Once again, there are countless opinions about what is the *right* or *wrong* method to use. However, there are two things you should keep in mind. Breakups are done at the comfort level of the person ending the relationship. You must also take into account the temperament of this person and the type of relationship you have had as well as its length. If you have personally witnessed him or her put their fist through a wall, throw furniture, or yell like a maniac when things did not go their way; it's probably not a good idea to break up in person. Do not concern yourself with your ex branding you as a coward. Your safety comes first. What your soon to be *ex* thinks of you is unimportant! You don't want to end up in one of those tragic news stories where someone is hurt badly or killed by the person they broke up with.

Under ordinary circumstances, you want to break up in person if possible. If you live apart gradually remove any items you have at their place *prior* to the day you have "the talk." On the actual day you plan to break up with them, make sure you have brought everything of theirs with you. Ideally you want to break up at *their place*. This allows you to exit after you have said what needs to be said as opposed to having to find a way to get them to leave your place. It is also safer for them to not have to drive right after you deliver news that is likely to upset them.

If you live together, find another place of your own or make arrangements in *advance* to have a place to go to after the conversation. Having to remain under the same roof after a breakup is living life on a high-tension wire without a net. If your name is on a lease you might schedule the breakup just prior to the deadline for renewing a new lease. Should you feel uncertain about your ability to *quietly* stay in the relationship until the lease expires before breaking up, review the consequences for breaking the lease. The cost of freedom is seldom too high. In the event you are married, it is advisable to meet with a divorce attorney or paralegal to get guidance.

If the relationship is a long distance, don't feel obligated to spend money flying to have the conversation nor should you allow them to invest their time and money coming out to visit you only to be shocked by your decision. Since you are the one ending the relationship, there should be no reason why _you aren't prepared. Anticipate how your future ex will respond to the news.

Execute

Keep the conversation short and to the point. You might say something along the lines of: "I've given this a lot of thought and I have reached the conclusion that I need to end our relationship." Expect to be asked (*Why?*), however, keep in mind there is no answer you can give that will put a smile on their face or cause them to feel you are making the *right decision*. The only answer to the *why* question is; "I'm not happy being in this relationship and I understand you are not responsible for my happiness. That is completely up to me."

Don't get sucked into a "blame game" or heated argument. The goal of your soon to be ex is to get you to list *reasons* which they'll try to convince you they can overcome or address. If you have honestly made up your mind the relationship is over, then it's simply cruel to allow them to beg, plead, or lose their dignity. You can also expect to be accused of never caring about

     The Breakup Method

them or of cheating. No one wants to believe they were dumped for being themselves. In their mind, something *underhanded* must have taken place. Stay calm!

Remember, it is not necessary to have a long drama filled nightmare discussion in order to justify a break up. If you are unhappy or want to date other people that is all the reason you need. In the event the conversation starts going sideways, make your exit while informing them you do not wish to be contacted for a while.

Move on and Allow Them to Get Over You

Do not offer "instant friendship" as a consolation prize. Too often people offer friendship in an attempt to avoid being looked at as "the bad guy." However, this tactic simply raises false hope for your ex that if they remain in your life there is a *chance,* they can *win you back* over time.

You are the last person who can help someone get over you! Remove yourself from their world as much as possible. Unfriend them on your social media, avoid places you know they frequent, block emails, texts, or calls. If you are sent gifts or cards, don't acknowledge them. The purpose of sending you things is to get *you to reply to them* or pull you back in. It is best to go "no contact" for six months to a year. The best friendships between exes usually occur when there has been a major gap in time and both people have become involved with others.

The goal is to
find a soulmate
not a cellmate...
**Suffering is
optional.**

The Upside of Divorce

I struggled with whether or not to write this chapter. Without a doubt, there will be some readers who will mistake what I am about to say as being a promotion to end marriages. I believe life is a personal journey and each of us is entitled to have our own "deal breakers." There are those who would tell you they don't believe in divorce. They also espouse the belief that every marriage can be "fixed" if a couple is willing to put in the work, communicate, and seek couples counseling to address difficult issues.

With regard to "work," I personally define it as doing one activity when you would rather be doing something else. Now, "a labor of love" is a completely different state of mind. The difference is you are putting in the effort because you want to maintain something *you* want.

A happy marriage is usually the result of two people coming together who want the same things and are in agreement on to how to obtain them. The key is to know yourself *before* merging your life with someone else.

Over the years, I have come to realize that problem relationships are for the most part not about accessing *right* or *wrong* but rather determining if you *agree* or *disagree*. Ultimately each of us is looking for someone who *naturally agrees* with us concerning the major things in life.

Divorce and Second Chances

If we strip away the emotional pain and oftentimes financial turmoil from the divorce process, it is nothing more than acknowledging a mistake has been made. One or both people have determined they need to change course in order to live a happier and more fulfilling life.

The purpose of divorce, bankruptcy, and amendments is to offer us an opportunity to have a second chance or make modifications in our life. Even with our legal system, we allow the majority of people who have committed crimes to get out of jail at some point.

Making mistakes from time to time is part of being human. Forcing someone to be stuck for the rest of their life because of a decision they made at age 19, 21, or whenever is to limit that person's ability to learn, evolve, and grow as an individual.

No one gets married planning to get divorced but it's good to know the law allows us the option to get out if we discover we've made a mistake in our mate selection process.

If it were no such thing as divorce, there would be fewer people taking a chance on marriage.

It's Like Breathing Fresh Air!

It's not uncommon for people to "find themselves" or rediscover passion concerning hobbies/interests and friendships they may have neglected or sacrificed in order to fit into a marriage that discouraged them from being their "authentic self."

Staying married for the wrong reasons is just as bad as getting married for the wrong reasons. Neither marriage nor divorce should be taken lightly.

This is *your* life. Don't let fear of the unknown or the opinions of others determine which road to take in your personal journey. Whatever you decide, there will be days of sunshine and days of rain. Only you can determine if a grave mistake has been made or a simple adjustment is needed. Use everything you learn to become the best you possible.

You are responsible for your own happiness.

Know yourself, love yourself, and trust yourself!

"**Nothing** Kills a **Dream** Like **Low Self- Esteem.**"

– Dr. Bruce Thiessen

New Beginnings

At some point, everyone after a breakup or divorce eventually gets back out into the dating scene. Oftentimes the thought of doing so can cause anxiety or apprehension. The following is in response to some questions posed to me by a journalist writing an article concerning first dates after having met someone using an online dating site.

What can you do to calm your anxiety when you're meeting the person you've been communicating with using an online dating site for the very first time?

Change Your Mindset

It's human nature to make it about you, and when you do, you fall into a "seller's mindset." A *seller* is always worried about his or her presentation and contemplating how they will overcome potential objections. A person with a "buyer's mindset" is evaluating qualities or traits to determine whether or not a product or person meets *their criteria.* Buyers are rarely nervous.

Keep Your Options Open

Engage with multiple people as opposed to putting all your eggs into one basket. If you feel *everything* is riding on a single date, you're going to be nervous. If you were seeking employment, you wouldn't stop sending out resumes just because you had a couple great phone interviews with *one* company!

Focusing on one person and behaving as if you're already in an *exclusive relationship* also puts you at risk of getting hurt especially if you are *ghosted* later. Keeping your options open by engaging with and dating multiple people helps prevent you from becoming *emotionally invested* too quickly with someone you barely know.

One of the main purposes of dating is to determine whether or not someone might be exclusive relationship material. Don't act as if you're already a couple! It's also wise to remember anyone who is *maintaining an active dating profile* is most likely engaging with others and keeping their options open, and so should you! Until an offer has been made and accepted, both the candidate and the company are within their rights to have *interviews* with others.

"Dating is primarily a numbers game.... People usually go through a lot of people to find good relationships. That's just the way it is." - Henry Cloud

Make Having A Good Time Your Goal

No one is asking you to decide on whether to cut *the red wire* or *the blue wire*. It's just a date!

Plan on enjoying; the meal, play, movie, concert, festival, picnic, or whatever else the date entails. Ideally, you should have established a good rapport over the phone by having had verbal conversations, text exchanges, and shared a few laughs. In the event you have not done so, there is a good chance you have agreed to meet too soon.

Dating without having established a good rapport with someone is almost the equivalent of being a salesperson making cold calls door to door. Never go out with anyone you don't feel some level of comfort with. To do otherwise increases your chances of having awkward or bad first dates.

What can you do before or during the date to relax?

Don't Say Yes to Every Dating Opportunity

Make sure you've established a good rapport. Generally speaking, if there has been no chemistry on the phone, there most likely will not be any chemistry in person. Going on dates whenever you have an opportunity including those times when you're not really in the mood just leads to *dating burnout*. It's okay to say *no* when you're really *not feeling it*. Many are called but *few* are chosen.

Daytime Is the Right Time for a First Date

While most people consider night dates to be more romantic, daytime dates are usually far safer.
Going out to breakfast, a brunch, a lunch, a festival, or similar outing, allows both people to dress casually and also be more relaxed. Daytime dating activities tend to be less alcohol fueled and generally conclude long before bedtime which eliminates a lot of seduction efforts.

Pick the Place

Oftentimes, the first few dates are met with a certain amount of indecisiveness regarding *where* to go or *what* to do. If your proposed date asks you what *you* would like to do or where *you* would like to go, *pick a place you enjoy and feel safe*. Being in a familiar place and engaging in an activity you enjoy is not only safer but also increases the chances you'll have a good time.

Meet and Greet for the First Date

For safety precautions, it is best for each person to have their own transportation and agree to meet at the designated location. When you agree to meet at a place, no one has to know where anyone lives and you are free to leave whenever *you* feel like it.

Call a Friend

Always make sure you let a friend or family member know you have a date planned, the time, with whom, and where. You may even arrange to have them call you or send you a text to check in with you an hour or two into the date. You should forewarn your date early on that you're expecting a call so as not to appear rude for taking the call.

Keep Things Light

Dating is supposed to be a *fun sociable activity* embarked upon by two people during their leisure time. Avoid interrogation style questions or investing too much time trying to eliminate them from possible relationship consideration. Whether you like their answers or not, no one wants to feel like they're on a *job interview* during their free time.

Secondly, if someone is attracted to you, they're going to do their best to avoid saying or doing anything which might *blow it* with you! Therefore, you can take a lot of the answers one gives you during the "infatuation phase" of dating a new person with a grain of salt.

First date questions should be more like *ice breakers* designed to get a person to *relax* and open up. The purpose of a first date is to find out how *compatible* you are and to determine if there is any *chemistry* between you. If either person feels as if they did *not* have a good

New Beginnings

time after the first date, there is a good chance there will not be a second date.

The following are topics and questions you can ask a person over *multiple* dates. Nevertheless, you don't want to monopolize conversations by asking one question after another. Hopefully, your date is interested in learning something about *you*. Being asked questions indicates interest.

Joys

How do you like to spend your weekends?
What type of music are you into?
What's your favorite ice cream flavor?
Would you describe yourself as being more of an introvert or an extrovert?
Given a chance, would you choose—a Sunday at home with family or out with your friends?
What's your favorite holiday and why?
What's your favorite movie/tv show or book?
What's your "go-to-pick me up" activity when you are feeling anxious or down?
What are your favorite pizza toppings and pizzeria?

Career

What type of person are you—"work to live" or "live to work?"
Are you happy where you are in your career at present?
What inspired you to get into your field of work?

How do you separate your personal life from your work life?

What's the worst job you have ever had?

Family

Were you close to your family while growing up?

Who is your "go-to-person" in your family when you are low?

What was it like growing up as the oldest/youngest/only child?

Which character trait do you share with your parents?

Values

What is the definition of success for you?

Do you consider yourself spiritual or religious?

Who inspires you the most in the world?

What attracts you to a person?

Is there any particular motto or piece of advice that you follow?

Do you believe in soulmates?

Do you believe in life after death?

Dreams

Do you regret not following any particular dreams?

What would be your three wishes if you had a genie?

Name a place you hope to travel to someday and why?

If you could change anything about your life, what would it be?

New Beginnings

What would you like to do if you found out this would be your last day on Earth?

Always Leave Them Wanting More

Avoid *marathon* first dates. They rarely lead to having a second date. A first date which lasts 2-3 hours is ideal. What normally happens beyond that is both people eventually get tired of talking or run out of things to say at some point and awkward silence appears. Once people feel as if they know everything there is to know about someone, they're not in a rush to see them again.

What can you do if you feel out of practice, especially when it comes to kissing, showing physical affection?

A Kiss to Remember

There are those who swear by never kissing on the first date. However, the kiss is what seals the deal with regard to whether or not you have chemistry. Kissing is like riding a bicycle. Over analyzing keeps one from allowing nature to take its course. Showing affection shouldn't be a paint by numbers kind of thing. If you're attracted to someone, feel chemistry, or are aroused by them, your body's sense memory will kick in. A passionate kiss will make a person dream about having the next date. On the other hand, if you're not feeling comfortable you shouldn't attempt to force yourself to kiss or be affectionate with anyone.

Trust Yourself

It's important to craft a mate selection/screening process and *must haves list* you believe in. When you distrust someone, you are in a relationship with, it ultimately means you don't trust your selection process to choose *the right person* for yourself. Never confuse fear with *red flags*.

"Maybe love is like luck. You have to go all the way to find it." - Robert Mitchum

Other Books by this Author

My Cat Won't Bark! (A Relationship Epiphany): *My Cat Won't Bark!* is about learning how to approach relationships with complete awareness, having realistic expectations, and using self-empowerment techniques. It is laced with several humorous anecdotes and has received noteworthy positive editorial reviews from the likes of Publishers Weekly, Reader's Favorite, and Midwest Book Review.

Online Dating Avoid the Catfish!: How to Date Online Successfully: *Avoid the Catfish!* is for anyone who wants to take control of their online dating endeavors.

"It's not that online dating sucks, too many people suck at online dating!"

Avoid the Catfish! is a must read for anyone considering using an online dating site or app!

Pump Your Brakes! How To Stop Having Bad First Dates: This book is designed to help readers keep things in perspective when it comes to first dates. Dating is supposed to be a *fun* sociable activity. This is especially true of a *first* date. The book is packed with dos and don'ts, along with how to deal with *ghosting* and finding your *ideal mate.*

"Never love anyone who treats you like you're ordinary." – Oscar Wilde